Getting to know the Bible

A Redemptorist Publication

Introduction

To encourage more people to read the Bible, St. Theresa's Parish in Birstall, Leicester, produced a **Bible Reading Scheme** which followed a path through the whole Bible in one year. The intention was to help each person to grow in confidence of approach to the Scriptures, knowing the pattern and outline of the Bible, and then, in succeeding years, to explore them ever more deeply.

This booklet is based on the outline programme prepared by their parish priest, Fr. John Daley. It can be used individually or in a group. A group may meet to read and discuss the outline introduction. Then, during the subsequent weeks, the particular book or books are read, studied, browsed through. If a little time can be set aside each day for reading the particular section the programme will prove both rewarding and enjoyable.

It will not be possible to read all of each section. However, the guide is so presented that the main passages of the Old Testament books are pointed out and the Gospels can be read thoroughly. The Deutero-canonical Books, which are not in all Bibles, are included.

In our reading of the Scriptures, our reflections and discussions, we may try to do all the work ourselves – and fail. The Holy Spirit, inspirer of the Scriptures, will guide us to all truth, as Jesus said.

**Come Holy Spirit,
fill the hearts of the faithful,
and kindle in us
the fire of your love.**

12 Month
Bible Reading Plan

Part One
The Gospel according to St Matthew

You will enjoy reading this Gospel account, aware of the love and reverence for the Old Testament that the writer feels and wants you to share, and of how he sees Jesus fulfilling all that the Old Testament promised God would do in the fullness of time.

The Gospel is in seven parts: (1) the birth and infancy of Jesus; (2-6) these five sections hold teachings and Jesus' missionary journeys and actions; (7) the passion, death and resurrection of Jesus. Seven is a Jewish mystical number, and you will notice it recurring time and again.

Chapter 1 Matthew traces the ancestry of Jesus from Abraham. There are six generations of seven names each. Jesus begins the seventh. Reassuringly, the story of Jesus' ancestry reflects the strengths, weaknesses and the variety to be found in most family histories.

Joseph does not feel worthy to marry Mary when he discovers that God has chosen her. The angel reassures him, and he marries her.

Chapter 2 A chapter fulfilling prophecies. The wise of the world acknowledge the birth of the saviour, and bring gold for a king, incense for a god, and myrrh for a burial. The flight into Egypt recalls Jacob and his family going there to escape famine, and another Joseph saved them (Genesis 37+). When danger is over the Holy Family return to the Promised Land.

Chapter 3 Begins over thirty years later. John the Baptist is preparing the way for Jesus, and baptises him.

Chapter 4 Jesus prepares himself for his ministry, calls his first disciples, and begins to preach and heal the sick.

Chapter 5 The sermon on the mount. Jesus spells out the beatitudes, and offers ideals higher than those of the Old Law.

Chapter 6 Do not show off your good deeds. Pray quietly. Trust in God, not in money.

Chapter 7 Do not judge others harshly. Be kind. Be sincere.

Chapter 8 Jesus works a range of miracles.

Chapter 9 More miracles, and he goes out to sinners.

Chapter 10 He sends the apostles on their first mission, having just chosen them from amongst his disciples.

Chapter 11 Jesus speaks of the kingdom of heaven to which people are invited now. He is sad that some people are not interested.

Chapter 12 The Pharisees challenge Jesus and the good work he is doing, even accusing him of being in league with Beelzebub, the prince of devils.

Chapter 13 Jesus speaks in parables. The disciples are puzzled. People do not understand. No-one had taught in parables before. Jesus explains that if people are sincere they will see the truth within the parables: if not, they will only hear a story.

Chapter 14 John the Baptist is executed. Jesus feeds the multitude (notice the numbers 7 & 12). He crosses the water dry-shod (remember Moses and the Israelites).

Chapter 15 Jesus challenges the traditions of the Pharisees, heals the foreigner's daughter and others. He feeds another multitude (notice the numbers 7 & 4. Not quite so complete as the first time, 7 & 12).

Chapter 16 Peter is blessed to see who Jesus truly is. The Pharisees and the Sadducees can't. Their opposition to him is harder. Jesus says he must be ready to suffer, and so must we if we follow him.

Chapter 17 The Transfiguration. Peter, James and John see Jesus with Moses and Elijah. They realise Jesus is the one Israel had longed for.

Chapter 18 Gentle, general advice. We are to reflect God's forgiveness to one another.

Chapter 19 A chapter of ideals. To be poor, faithful, chaste, for Christ.

Chapter 20 The Passion is nearer. The Apostles are to share his suffering. They are to serve. No-one is excluded from God's love (parable of labourers in the vineyard).

Chapter 21 Jesus enters Jerusalem, drives money-changers and dealers out of the Temple, and answers questions on his authority. Now he is in danger of arrest.

Chapter 22 Parable of the Wedding feast. Challenged by Pharisees and Sadducees, Jesus silences his challengers. He speaks the great commandment.

Chapter 23 Condemnation of the Pharisees.

Chapter 24 Jesus speaks of the end of the world, the destruction of Jerusalem, his death and resurrection.

Chapter 25 Parables of the bridesmaids, of the talents, and an image of the Last Judgement.

Chapter 26 The story of Jesus' passion begins. He is anointed at Bethany, has the Last Supper with his disciples, is arrested, and put on trial.

Chapter 27 Jesus before Pilate, crowned with thorns, crucified, dies and is buried. The tomb is guarded.

Chapter 28 The women come to the tomb, and give the message to the apostles to meet Jesus in Galilee. Jesus is risen. He sends them on their mission.

Part 2
The Book of
Genesis

Chapter 1 *Genesis* means "in the beginning", and a fascinating poem opens the Bible. The poet pictures God working over the six days and rests on the seventh. God shapes creation, then the world, then brings life to it. Finally, he creates human beings to be stewards of creation.

Chapter 2 A second, older, account of the creation of mankind. God creates man from the soil (we are made of the food we eat), and woman is given life from man. Neither person yet has a name.

Chapter 3 The man and woman are tempted to taste the fruit of the tree of the knowledge of good and evil, bringing evil into God's good world. They must bear the consequences of their choice, and will know suffering. The man gives his wife the name 'Eve', meaning 'mother'. Adam, 'made of soil', is the man's name.

Chapter 4 Cain and Abel are born, representing the farmer and the shepherd. The farmer kills the shepherd, an image of Israel's enemies slaying the Israelites, Cain flees from the land and becomes a stranger, marrying a wife in another country, the land of Nod, east of Eden. The Bible does not see Adam and Eve as the only first parents on earth.

These are powerful stories, holding religious truth. God created the world good. Humankind brought evil into it, and the evil even comes to murder when brother kills brother.

Chapter 5 Extraordinary ages of a distant past – patriarchs.

Chapter 6, 7, 8 The story of the Flood, or, rather, two stories intertwined. Human sin is so constant that God repents creation. Noah and his family are saved – human life still exists – so it must have been good. The ark holds creatures because they, too, have continued to exist. One story says a pair of each, the other says seven pairs of clean and one pair of unclean. There will be enough food – only clean animals could be eaten.

Chapter 9 The new creation. Noah and his family receive the

blessing man and woman received in chapter one. They are stewards of God's creation.

Chapter 10 The earth is peopled. Three tribes of peoples, descended from Noah's sons Japheth, Ham and Shem, spread over the world.

Chapter 11 The peoples plan a tower to reach and conquer heaven. God confuses their languages, and they cannot understand each other. They separate and go to their own lands.

This chapter ends the introduction to the Bible. Chapters 1-11 are full of great truths about God's creation, evil and its consequences, human pride, God's justifiable anger and forgiveness. The world, as the author of the Book of Genesis saw it, was full of evil and pride and division, and yet he still believed in a God who was good and wanted to love and bless his people. Human sin could thwart God's love but not destroy it. The author speaks of the world as he sees it, but in images of the past.

Chapter 12 Begins the story of Abraham. Abraham and Sarah are the parents of the Jewish people. God promises them a family and a great people.

Chapter 13 Abraham and Lot, his nephew, go their separate ways.

Chapter 14 Abraham brave and victorious. Melchizedek makes a mysterious appearance.

Chapter 15 God makes a Covenant with Abraham.

Chapter 16 Sarah gives Abraham her servant-girl. Desperate to have a child, she becomes jealous and drives away the girl.

Chapter 17 God promises the child he has spoken of will belong to Abraham and Sarah. The Covenant is confirmed.

Chapter 18 Sodom and Gomorrah are sinful. Abraham pleads for them.

Chapter 19 The two cities are destroyed.

Chapter 21 Isaac is born.

Chapter 22 Abraham is asked to sacrifice Isaac. The worship of the false god, Moloch, required the sacrifice of children – especially of the first-born. Would Abraham do for God what others did for Moloch?

The story of patriarch Isaac begins in **Chapter 24**. Jacob's story takes over in **28**, and in **37** the story of Joseph begins. Joseph's brothers are jealous of him and sell him into slavery. After suffering and imprisonment Joseph prospers and becomes important in Egypt. When famine strikes, food is plentiful in Egypt, so Jacob and his family are able to come to live there. The Book of Genesis ends with the deaths of Jacob and Joseph. Joseph had saved the family, the people, of Israel.

Part 3
The Books of Exodus, Leviticus, Numbers & Deuteronomy

The Book of Exodus is the second book of the Bible. It begins about 1250 B.C.

A cruel Pharaoh rules in Egypt. He has made slaves of the family of Jacob (Israel) and the Hebrew people cry out to God. God sends them a saviour, Moses, who leads the Israelites out of Egypt through the desert to the Promised Land – promised to Abraham and his descendants centuries before.

The story of the exodus from Egypt, through the desert, the giving of the Law, the reaching the Promised Land, is told in four books: Exodus, Leviticus, Numbers, Deuteronomy, and these, together with the Book of Genesis, make up the Pentateuch, the five books of the Law, the 'Torah'. Jesus came to fulfil the Law and the Prophets.

The Book of Exodus

Chapter 1 The Hebrews have become slaves.

Chapter 2 Moses is born. He is saved from death. He escapes from Egypt after killing an Egyptian.

Chapter 3 Moses a shepherd in the Sinai Desert. God speaks from the burning bush and gives Moses his mission.

Chapter 4 Moses' brother, Aaron, is chosen to help Moses because Moses does not speak well.

Chapter 5 Moses and Aaron approach the Pharaoh. He is angry and increases the sufferings of the Hebrew work-force. The Hebrews blame Moses and Aaron.

Chapter 7 The Plagues begin. They are intended to show the power of God working through Moses. The Plagues are all natural disasters, common in that part of the world, except the last one.

Chapter 11 The death of the first-born.

Chapter 12 The Passover. The Israelites celebrate the night they were rescued from Egypt.

Chapter 13 The Israelites must consecrate the first-born to God. They leave Egypt.

Chapter 14 The Egyptians pursue the Israelites who cross the sea of Reeds safely. Note the details of the miracle. The wind blows through the night, the tide goes out, the land is firm enough to walk on. We would call it providential, the Israelites see God's hand more directly and call it miraculous.

Chapter 15 They sing with joy, then grumble at having no water.

Chapter 16 & 17 The people are hungry and thirsty. They protest. God provides.

Chapter 18 Moses is advised by Jethro, his father-in-law.

Chapter 19 The Israelites come to Mount Sinai, in that part of the desert where Moses had been shepherding when God spoke to him from the burning bush. God promises a Covenant. The people pray. God comes to the mountain on the third day, and Moses goes into the cloud of God's presence to speak to him.

Chapter 20 God gives the Commandments. There follows the details of Law.

Chapter 32 The people tire of waiting. They make a golden calf to worship. Moses is angry and smashes to the ground the tablets of stone, upon which God had written. Moses punishes the people.

Chapter 34 Moses ascends Mount Sinai again, and God gives the Law once more. But this time Moses writes it on the stone.

Chapter 35 and following. Details of the building and furnishing of the sanctuary.

The Book of Leviticus is a book of laws. You may find it difficult to read, even boring. Browse, and see what you find.

The Book of Numbers opens with four chapters of names, continues with various laws, and begins the journey through the wilderness again.

Chapter 11 Moses finds the complaints of the Israelites hard to bear.

Chapter 12 Even Aaron and Miriam, his brother and sister, criticise Moses.

Chapter 13 They approach the Promised Land. A member of each tribe is sent to reconnoitre the land. It is beautiful, but the people in possession would be too strong to battle against.

Chapter 14 The pilgrim people lose heart. God has failed them. They will never be able to take possession of the land. God is angry and says he will not allow them to conquer. Against Moses' advice the Israelites go into battle, but are heavily defeated.

Chapter 15 More laws follow. Then come the strange stories of the Waters of Meribah (20) the Bronze Serpent (21) and Balaam and his donkey (22, 24).

More chapters of law bring the book to an end.

The Book of Deuteronomy is the final book of the Law, the Torah. Moses gathers the people around him. He knows he is soon to die, and wants to tell the people how good God has been to them. He recalls the details of the journey through the wilderness, and reminds them of the laws God gave to guide his people. The word *Deuteronomy* means a second telling. Browse through the book, and note God's love and the appeal to be faithful (chapters 5, 6, 7), the laws on killing and war (19 & 20), on marriage and faithfulness (21 & 22), God's Covenant (30), the death of Moses (34).

Part 4
The historical Books of Joshua, Judges, Ruth, Samuel and Kings, Chronicles, Ezra and Nehemiah, & Maccabees

These books cover a period of hundreds of years. You will find parts of the story fascinating, bewildering, revolting – it is human life and history. God is watching his people develop. We want him to intervene, to stop the cruelty and suffering, and we are astounded that God's people can be so cruel and evil. Then we remember that we are the same now – a world in which there is much suffering that we inflict on one another. Does God care? We believe he does. He loves and suffers with us, helpless against the freedom he has given us. We are free to choose good or evil. God will not take away that freedom – but he will guide us.

Joshua

Chapter 2 The story of Rahab.

Chapter 3 The people cross the River Jordan.

Chapter 6 Jericho is conquered, and cruelly put under the ban.

Chapter 9 The peculiar treaty with the Gibeonites.

Chapter 11 & 12 Joshua conquers the land.

Chapter 13-19 The tribes of Israel are given their territorial land.

Chapter 20 Cities of Refuge.

Chapter 24 Joshua retells their story before he dies.

Judges

The *Judges* were the leaders of the people in difficult times. Chapter 2 tells the story briefly. Browse through the book, but do read about Deborah (Chapter 4), Gideon (Chapters 6 & 7) and the story of Samson which begins in Chapter 13.

Ruth

A beautiful short story. Ruth was in the family line of Jesus – her son, Obed, was the grandfather of King David.

I Samuel

This book opens early in the 11th Century B.C. and tells the story of the prophets, Samuel's family, and especially of his mother's longing to have a child.

Chapter 1 Hannah's longing and prayer.

Chapter 2 Hannah rejoices at the birth of her son.

Chapter 3 God calls Samuel. Samuel grows to greatness, but the people ask for a King rather than a prophet to lead them.

Chapter 10 Samuel anoints Saul as King.

Chapter 15 The strange story of Saul's displeasing God, and losing his favour.

Chapter 16 Saul chooses and anoints David.

Chapter 17 David defeats Goliath.

Chapter 18 Saul is Jealous.

Chapter 22 David flees for his life, and becomes an outlaw.

Chapters 23 & 24 Saul pursues David. David has an opportunity to kill the King.

Chapter 31 King Saul dies in battle.

II Samuel

Chapter 1 David laments the deaths of Saul and Jonathan. Jonathan had been David's closest friend, even though he was son of Saul.

Chapter 2-5 David becomes King of Israel and then of Judah. This unites the two kingdoms.

Chapter 7 David longs to thank God, and God blesses and reassures him.

Chapter 11 David sins by taking Bathsheba, the wife of Uriah, and then plotting Uriah's death.

Chapter 12 God rebukes David through the prophet Nathan. The child dies. Bathsheba conceives again, and gives birth to Solomon.

Chapter 13-20 David's son Absalom plots and revolts against his father. The rebellion succeeds at first, but is then defeated.

Chapter 22 David sings a psalm of triumph and gratitude.

Chapter 24 A strange chapter. David displeases God, but it is the people who suffer.

I Kings

Chapter 1 David is dying. Bathsheba and Nathan plot for Solomon to become King.

Chapter 3 Solomon is King. He asks God to give him wisdom. He shows wisdom in a judgement that pleases the people.

Chapter 5-8 Solomon builds the temple, and a palace for himself.

Chapter 10 Visit of the Queen of Sheba.

Chapter 11 Solomon's wives and concubines and enemies. Solomon dies.

Chapter 12 His son Roboam succeeds him, but Jeroboam revolts against him. The kingdom divides into Israel and Judah.

Chapter 17 In the middle of the ninth century B.C., Elijah appears as God's prophet in Israel. God looks after his prophet in time of drought. Elijah heals the widow's son.

Chapter 18 Elijah proves the truth of God.

Chapter 19 He travels to Mount Horeb to meet God. This is Mount Sinai where, so many centuries before, God had given the law to Moses. It is God's mountain.

Chapter 21 Ahab and Jezebel are evil – King and Queen.

II Kings

Chapter 2 Elijah is taken up to Heaven, Elisha succeeds him. He works miracles.

Chapter 4-5 More miracles of Elisha. The rest of the Second Book of Kings tells the story of the Kings of Israel and Judah. You may find it interesting to browse through them. Typical of the cruelty of the time is chapter 10 & 11. Chapter 17, the Assyrians invade and conquer Israel in 721 B.C. and create Samaria. The Samaritans become hated by the people of Judah and Israel.

The prophet Isaiah appears in Judah, 740. He helps the King and people stand firm against the Assyrians, and especially helps and advises Hezekiah (chapter 20). But succeeding Kings are unfaithful to God, except for Josiah who tries to win the people back to God (22 & 23). After his reign the kingdom collapses and is invaded by the Babylonians. Jerusalem destroyed and the people taken into exile (587 B.C.).

The Book of Chronicles tell much of the story of the Books of Samuel & Kings.

The Books of Ezra & Nehemiah tell the story of the return from exile in 538 and the building up once more of the Community of God's people.

The Books of Maccabees take us up to the years before Christ. They concern the Jewish struggle for religious and political independence.

24

Part 5
The Gospel according to Mark

This seems to be the earliest of the Gospel accounts, though many scholars believe there was an early edition of Matthew (perhaps about 45-50 A.D.) from which the fuller Gospel was written about 70-80 A.D. Luke's Gospel is about the same time, or a few years later, and Mark's is dated 60-65, possibly written when Mark was with Peter in Rome. We would like clearer information, but the Roman persecutions included the destruction of Church documents, part of the demoralisation of the Christian Community – a denying of their history.

Mark's Gospel does not have a clear plan or structure as the others do. Matthew has an introduction (Infancy narratives), then five sections of narrative and instruction, then passion, death and resurrection. Luke has an introduction (Infancy narratives) and then Jesus' travelling around Galilee (4-9), a journey to Jerusalem (9-19), a Jerusalem ministry (19-21) and the passion, death and resurrection. John's Gospel has a Prologue and an Opening Week, and then is structured on the feasts of the Jewish People: Passover, Sabbath, Passover, Tabernacles, Dedication, Passover – with the passion, death and resurrection.

Mark

Chapter 1 John is preaching and baptising at the River Jordan. Jesus is baptised, begins to preach, calls the first of his disciples, cures the sick.

Chapter 2 Forgives and cures a paralysed man. Calls Matthew (Levi), mixes with sinful people, and there is rivalry with John the Baptist's disciples and troubles with the Pharisees.

Chapter 3 Jesus carries on healing, chooses his 12 Apostles from amongst the disciples, is accused of being in league with the devil. His relatives are worried about him. He says we can all be his relatives.

Chapter 4 A chapter of parables. The disciples are confused, do not understand preaching of the parables. Jesus seems to answer that the parables are a test: the genuine listener will learn the truth, others will only hear a story.

Chapter 5 Jesus heals the possessed man. Notice how much better Mark tells the story than does Matthew, and the same with the healing of Jairus' daughter and the woman suffering from a haemorrhage. Luke's is not so good as Mark's either. Puzzle: if Mark's account is the first and best, why didn't Matthew and Luke simply copy it?

Chapter 6 Jesus comes home to Nazareth, sends his Apostles on their first mission. Herod is afraid. He fears Jesus may be John the Baptist come back to life. Jesus feeds a multitude with five loaves and two fish, and walks on water. The events recall Moses and Manna in the desert and the Crossing of the Sea of Reeds.

Chapter 7 The Old and New in contrast here. Jesus is seen as unfaithful. He heals again – foreigners this time. Has he come for the whole world?

Chapter 8 A second feeding of a multitude. It happens after three days. There are seven loaves, four thousand people, seven basketfuls left over. Just as in Matthew's Gospel account. Luke does not have this story. Did he think there was only one miraculous feeding of the crowd? A blind man is cured in stages. Why? The Pharisees ask for a sign. Jesus asks for followers – and says the call is absolute.

Chapter 9 The Transfiguration. The Apostles realise who Jesus is, but they are not to tell anyone yet. He says more: John the Baptist had been the "new Elijah", preparing the way for the Messiah. To be great in God's eyes we must be humble.

Chapter 10 Jesus speaks of divorce and restates the ideal that God gave at the beginning of Creation. Children are blessed. The rich young man is interested, but turns away. Riches are a danger. Jesus speaks of his Passion again, but the disciples do not understand. John and James want to be important, and there is rivalry amongst the apostles. Jesus heals a blind man. Puzzle: Mark says "as he left Jericho" and calls him Bartimaeus; Luke says "before he entered Jericho" but mentions no name; Matthew says there were two blind men. Three traditions of the one event?

Chapter 11 Jesus enters Jerusalem, expels the traders from the Temple, curses the barren fig tree. Was the "fig tree" originally a story that became an event, or a dramatic parable-in-action such as we read in the books of the prophets of the Old Testament?

Chapter 12 The wicked husbandmen. Tribute to Caesar. Resurrection from the dead. The Great Commandment. The widow's mite.

Chapter 13 The destruction of Jerusalem is an image of the end of the world. There are signs in every age that the world will come to an end. "Be on your guard, stay awake."

Chapter 14 Jesus is anointed at Bethany, two days before the Passover. Two days? John says it was six days. What day was the Last Supper? Jesus eats the Last Supper with his disciples. Institutes the Eucharist. Suffers in the Garden of Gethsemane, is arrested and brought before the Sanhedrin. Peter denies him.

Chapter 15 Jesus before Pilate. Crowned with thorns, carries the cross. He is crucified at 9.00 in the morning. What day was he arrested? Jesus dies. He is wrapped in a shroud and laid in a tomb.

Chapter 16 The women find the tomb empty. They are so frightened they tell no-one what they have seen. Jesus shows himself several times in the course of that day, and ascends to Heaven. Read again how the other Gospel accounts relate what happened on the day of the Resurrection. You will discover that you cannot say who went to the tomb, nor with certainty

at what time, nor when the spices were bought and prepared…
and that the shroud of Friday afternoon has become the burial
cloths of Sunday morning. Fascinating, isn't it? So… what
happened? Who told the story first? Why the differences? The
Church has not been worried or concerned about the
differences. Need we be? Some people find them disturbing,
whilst others see them as a reason to dismiss the whole story.
The faith in the Risen Lord is what shines through all the
accounts.

Part 6
The
Old Testament
Prophets

A prophet is someone inspired by God to speak to the people. It may be to warn them of the evil in their lives, to remind them of a God loving and true, to point out the errors of their ways, to encourage them in difficult times. The prophet speaks always of God and his blessings – past, present, future – and therefore always looks forward to a time of peace and blessing beyond any suffering that has to be endured.

Moses was the first of the prophets, and the line runs down to John the Baptist and Jesus. Names like Gad and Nathan (in the time of King David) Elijah and Elisha (in the times of Ahab and Jezebel) occur in the historical books. But there are also books of the prophets – Isaiah, Jeremiah and Ezekiel are among the most celebrated.

Isaiah

Isaiah was called to be a prophet in 740 B.C. He gives an account of the call in chapter 6, and an understanding of God's love and invitation even in the mother's womb comes in chapter 49. His mission was to bring Israel and Judah from infidelity to the right way.

You will find the book has three parts: 1-39, 40-55 written much later, and 56-66 a completion by a third author, but you will feel a unity of the whole work: it is the spirit of Isaiah.

Chapter 1 God asks the people to be true to him.

Chapter 2 A lovely vision of peace.

Chapter 5 The song of the vineyard.

Chapter 6 Isaiah is called.

Chapter 7 Ahaz is fearful. Isaiah reassures him. The virgin will bear a child.

Chapter 9 A child is born for us.

Chapter 11 The Jesse Tree. Salvation will come.

Chapter 24 Terrifying images of defeat.

Chapter 25 Peace, thanksgiving, the Messianic Banquet which becomes an image of Eternal life.

Chapter 35 There will be a return from exile and the joy of resettlement.

Chapter 38 Hezekiah is about to die. He sings a powerful lament, but it ends in the joy of recovery.

Chapter 40 The Book of Consolation of Israel begins. The prophet is coming to speak God's peace.

Chapter 41 Do not fear.

Chapter 42 The servant of Yahweh comes.

Chapter 49 The servant sings a song of rejoicing. He was chosen even from the womb to sing God's glory.

Chapter 50 The third song.

Chapter 53 The fourth song. The servant suffers and dies, but Yahweh will raise him and we shall share his glory.

Chapter 55 A final chapter of Consolation.

Chapter 58 Be true to God.

Chapter 60 The new Jerusalem is a sign for all nations.

Chapter 61 The prophet's vocation.

Chapter 63 A psalm to the Lord's goodness.

Jeremiah

Jeremiah, born about a hundred years later than Isaiah, 646 B.C., was called at the age of twenty, and suffered mockery, imprisonment, torture. He was a failure. Only after his death was his goodness appreciated.

Chapter 1 The call of Jeremiah – even before being conceived.

Chapter 2 The people have deserted God.

Chapter 3 Be converted, repent.

Chapter 10 Worship God, not idols.

Chapter 13 Parable-in-action: the loin-cloth.

Chapter 15 God speaks like this?

Chapter 18 Another parable-in-action: the potter.

Chapter 19 Yahweh and Jeremiah speak.

Chapter 20 Jeremiah finds life unbearable.

Chapter 24 Vision of the baskets of figs.

Chapter 25 Babylon will conquer Judah and Jerusalem.

Chapter 26 Jeremiah asks the people to relent. They condemn him.

Chapter 30 A chapter of consolation for Israel and Judah.

Chapter 31 Joy on the return from exile.

Ezekiel

Ezekiel spent his life as a prophet among the exiles in Babylon. Jerusalem fell in the year 587, and Ezekiel went into exile having failed to influence the people 591-87 (chapter 4-24). He speaks against the nations that have drawn Israel from God (chapter 25-32), speaks comfort for the future, (33-39), and lays plans for the re-establishment of Israel (40-48).

Chapter 1 The chariot of Yahweh.

Chapter 2 Ezekiel eats the word of God.

Chapter 3 He is struck dumb.

Chapter 4 & 5 Parables-in-action.

Chapter 16 An extraordinary chapter. Israel is a wife that became a harlot.

Chapter 17 The Eagle.

Chapter 18 Individual responsibility.

Chapter 23 Another chapter like 16. Jerusalem and Samaria unfaithful.

Chapter 24 Jerusalem besieged. Ezekiel's wife dies.

Chapter 25-32 Ezekiel speaks against the nations and especially Egypt: the Cedar (31) and Crocodile (32).

Chapter 34 The shepherds of Israel have failed the people.

Chapter 40-48 Plans for the future.

Many Books of Prophets are brief but they are not less significant for that. You will enjoy browsing through them. What follows now is what "not to miss" as a thread for your reading.

Daniel

Chapters 1-6 Daniel is a visionary and an interpreter of dreams.

Chapter 13 Daniel saves Susannah.

Chapter 14 Daniel in the lions' den again.

Hosea

The prophets wife is unfaithful but he wins back her love: just as God wins unfaithful Israel (chapter 1-3).

Chapter 11 God is desolate.

Chapter 14 Hosea appeals to the people.

Jonah

The story is short but powerful. Jonah is a reluctant prophet who wants God only for the Chosen People, but God wants his love and forgiveness to go to everyone. God wins and Jonah is angry.

Micah

Chapter 4 Foresees the conversion of the nations.

Chapter 5 Bethlehem will be the birth-place of the chosen one.

Zephaniah

Chapter 3 The promises.

Zechariah

Chapter 1-8 speaks a number of visions.

Chapter 9 The Messiah is foretold and Israel restored.

Part 7
The Wisdom Books, Job, Psalms, Proverbs, Ecclesiastes, Song of Songs, Wisdom & Ecclesiasticus

37

You will enjoy the variety of this section of the Bible. The Psalms will delight and yet puzzle you with their beautiful poetry, extraordinary range of thought and feeling: startling directness towards God, his creation and life on earth. Wisdom, Proverbs, Ecclesiastes and Ecclesiasticus will amuse you and challenge you with their apt and pointed comments, and set you thinking as you recognise how true their judgements are. But the most powerful of the Wisdom Books is Job – a beautifully told story exploring the meaning of human suffering and the search for truth.

Job

Job is a good man, prosperous and happy, and grateful to God for his blessings.

God speaks in praise of Job to Satan who says he will prove Job's goodness is hollow. Notice that the name 'Satan' means an opponent. Job loses everything – his children, his possessions, but he remains faithful to God. Then he suffers illness. His friends (Job's comforters) tell him he must have done wrong to be punished like this, but Job knows he is innocent and argues against them. Read especially his words in **Chapters 7, 10, 14, 19.**

Chapter 32 Elihu speaks of the majesty and justice of God. The friends of Job had spoken in ignorance, Job himself nearer to the truth, but all falling short of true understanding.

Chapters 38, 39, 40 God himself speaks from the heart of the storm, and his questions are overwhelming. Job is reverently quiet. The story ends strangely in Chapter 42.

Psalms

You will be tempted to turn the pages and read the occasional short psalm. But don't miss all the longer psalms. Here is a selection you will enjoy, but you may well make your own better selection… **Psalm 8, 13, 14, 15, 19, 22, 23, 25, 33, 51, 53, 63, 84, 86, 90, 104, 110, 111, 112, 113, 116, 119, 123, 128, 130, 139, 138.** (N.B. The numbering of the Psalms may vary according to the version of the Bible you are using.)

Proverbs

Chapter 3 A father advises his son.

Chapter 4 Choose Wisdom.

Chapter 5 Be faithful and wise in love.

Chapter 6 Be honest, work industriously.

Chapter 8 (vv 22-31) Wisdom helped God at the Creation.

Chapter 9 Lady Wisdom and Dame Folly.

Chapters 10-22 are a collection of proverbs. Browse, and you will enjoy them.

Chapters 23-24 continue a series of wise sayings.

Chapters 25-29 More proverbs.

Chapter 31 The Perfect Wife.

Ecclesiastes

Ecclesiastes is a short book written by a seeming pessimist. He sees little of value in human life, everything fades. Belief in God is there, but life on earth is not seen as a blessing but rather as futile. Only glimpses of happiness are given. There is no understanding of why human life exists.

Song of Songs

Song of Songs is a love poem. Read it as one. It is also an allegory of the love God has for Israel and Israel for God. The prophets spoke of God's love for his people as that of a husband or lover: and this song expresses the same theme. There are five poems, and the voices are the Bride, the Bridegroom and the Chorus.

Wisdom

The author sees Wisdom as God's partner, with him at all times, guiding and blessing Creation. You will enjoy Chapters 1-9 especially, but you may find the rest of the book too historical.

Chapter 1 Seek God.

Chapter 2 Non-believers look at life.

Chapters 3, 4, 5 Better to believe in God.

Chapter 6 Advice on seeking Wisdom.

Chapter 7 Solomon as an ordinary man blessed with Wisdom by God. So may we be.

Chapter 8 Wisdom is precious.

Chapter 9 Prayer for Wisdom.

Chapter 10 Begins a historical survey of God and Wisdom, from Adam to Moses.

Chapter 11 Israel in Egypt.

Chapter 12 Other nations worshipped false gods.

Chapter 13, 14, 15 Nature cults and idols.

Chapter 16 Begins a heavy comparison between Israel and Egypt which completes the book. The author is grateful that God protects and guides Israel.

Ecclesiasticus

You will smile at the preface where the translator speaks of how difficult a task it is to edit and translate a book.

Chapters 1, 2 Wisdom and fear of God.

Chapter 3 Love your parents, be humble.

Chapter 4 Be kind and a person of integrity.

Chapter 5 Beware of money.

Chapter 6 Be a good friend.

Chapters 7, 8 Good general advice.

Chapter 9 Advice for men.

Chapter 13 Beware of social climbing.

Chapter 17 Remember God.

Chapter 18 God is all, we are so little.

Chapter 20 Watch your tongue.

Chapter 22 Wisdom and folly.

Chapters 25, 26 Women and wives.

Chapter 28 Watch your tongue.

Chapter 30 Bringing up children.

Chapter 34 On dreams and travelling.

Chapter 37 Asking advice.

Chapter 42 A father worries about his daughter.

Chapter 51 A hymn of thanksgiving and a search for wisdom.

There is so much to read in the Wisdom books. You will enjoy exploring. You cannot hope to read all the above in a month – but you will have a glimpse of what is there. You have the whole of your life to discover the riches of the Word of God.

Part 8
The Letters of
St Paul

43

St Paul was about twenty when Jesus began his ministry, but he never heard Jesus speak or even saw him. He was an ardent Jew, and seems to have hated the new Christian faith. He helped in the persecution of the Christians, but, on the road to Damascus in Syria, God called him in an extraordinary way. There was blinding light and a voice that asked Paul "Why do you persecute me?" It was Jesus. Paul's life changed. He became a Christian, lived quietly for some years, and then became an apostle. He made three missionary journeys through the Roman Empire, preaching Christ and writing letters to the communities he helped found. He was persecuted, just as he had persecuted, was imprisoned and tortured and finally executed. He lived and died for Christ.

His friend was St Luke. They travelled some of the missionary road together, and Luke writes about that in the "Acts of the Apostles". But we learn more about Paul from his letters, sent to the communities he had helped establish by his preaching. The letters reflect his concern for the people, his love of God, his belief in Christ, and his growth in all these as years went by. Paul received his faith in Christ as a gift on the road to Damascus, but by his love and living the faith his understanding of it developed.

Paul's Letters
Romans (57-58 A.D.)

1 Thanksgiving and prayer. Jesus has rescued us from sin (justification), from pagan ways. **2** The Law will not save us. **3** Nor even believing in God's promises. Faith in the Law must become faith in Christ. **4** Abraham's faith. **5** Salvation. Christ delivers us from Adam's sin. **6** Baptism. **7** Christians not bound by Old Testament Law. The spiritual struggle. **8** Christian spiritual life. We are children of God. **9 & 10** Israel has failed to see God has fulfilled his promise. **11** The Jews are still the Chosen People. They will be converted. **12** Be humble and charitable.

13 Obey lawful authority. 14 Be gentle with the scrupulous. 15 Be united. 16 Paul explains why he had never visited Rome, but now plans to. 17 A chapter of greetings and personal messages.

1 Corinthians (57 A.D.)

1 Paul disturbed by divisions at Corinth. 2 Paul preaches Christ, not human wisdom. 3 Christians should be united. Preachers serve God, do not create factions, looks for popularity. 5 There has been incest in the community. 6 Avoid pagan courts. Avoid fornication. 7 Marriage and virginity. Be at peace. 8 Food sacrificed to idols. 9 Paul speaks of himself as an apostle: self sacrificing, seeking only to serve God and his people. 10 Remember the past – no turning to idolatry. 11 Decorum in Public Worship. Be united, not divided into rich and poor. Ladies to be quiet. 12, 13, 14 Spiritual gifts within the community. The greatest is love. 15 The Resurrection. 16 Greetings and a promise to visit.

2 Corinthians

1 He apologises for changing his plans. He had not been able to visit. 2 Let there be forgiveness and reconciliation. 3 A Christian is a letter from Christ. 4 The apostles are weak, but God is with them. 5 Christ is all, and we are his ambassadors. 6 & 7 Paul spoke frankly in his first letter. He has no regrets. 8 & 9 Corinthians asked to be generous. God loves a cheeful giver. 10 Paul denies being weak or ambitious. 11 Paul boasts. 12 God asks him to suffer, and will be with him in his weakness. 13 Test yourselves. Are you genuine Christians?

Galatians (57-58 A.D.)

This is a severe letter. The Galatians have fallen away from Paul's teaching. He rebukes them. 1 God chose him (Paul) as an apostle to bring the Good News. 2 Council at Jerusalem decided

Christians were free of the Old Law. **3** Faith in Christ brings justification. **4** We are children of God. Contrast between Old and New Testaments (Hagar and Sarah). **5** Christian freedom in the Spirit. **6** Be kind and persevere in the faith.

Ephesians (61-63 A.D.)

The letter opens with a beautiful hymn to God in praise of the salvation brought us by Christ. **2** This salvation is a gift for everyone. Jew and Gentile, the whole world. **3** Paul prays that he be worthy of preaching this mystery. **4** Be united in the new life Christ has brought. **5** Reflect God's love, especially in the home. **6** Be courageous in faith.

Philippians (56-57 A.D.)

This is Paul's friendliest letter. He wrote it from prison. **1** He begins with prayer and thanksgiving, and says he is in prison – longing to die to be with Christ, yet ready to live on if that pleases God more. **2** Be humble as Jesus was. **3** Be willing to lose everything for the sake of Christ. **4** May you always be happy.

Colossians (61-63 A.D.)

1 I pray for you and am glad to suffer for you. **2** You have made some errors. **3** Be united with Christ and live good lives. **4** Bits of news.

1 Thessalonians (50-51 A.D.)

This is Paul's first letter. **1** God loves you. **2** Paul gave them good example when with them. **3** Timothy – he speaks well of them. **4** Be holy. We shall all be together after death. **5** Live a good life, ready to die. Be at peace.

2 Thessalonians (50-51 A.D.)

1 Be worthy of God's love. **2** The coming of Jesus at the end of time. **3** Don't be idle. Work steadily. Don't be a burden on others.

1 Timothy

Timothy was a friend and fellow apostle. He was bishop of Ephesus. **1** Speak against false teachings. **2** The worshipping assembly – prayer and the place of women. **3** Choose elders and deacons carefully. **4** Oppose false teachers. **5** Protect and look after widows. **6** Serve your community wisely.

2 Timothy

1 You have been blessed. **2** Be courageous. **3** Watch out for false Christians. **4** I shall soon die. Carry on the good work.

Titus

Another friend of Paul, Bishop of Crete. **1** Appoint elders wisely, oppose false teachers. **2** Moral guidance. **3** Christians to be kind.

Philemon

This letter is a plea for an escaped prisoner named Onesimus.

Did you find the letters of St Paul exhausted you? You will have caught the flavour of his energy and zeal, and the depth of his thought.

Part 9
The Gospel according to St Luke

Luke writes a short introduction. He has carefully looked at all sources available to him preparing to write this account of Jesus' life and ministry. He addresses Theophilus, a name which means "loved by God". It probably means you and me (and everyone) – "Dear Reader".

Luke was a friend of St Paul. They travelled together on missionary journeys. He wrote the gospel some years after St Paul's death, round about the year 80 A.D. (Matthew's account was written about 75 A.D. (though there was probably an earlier shorter version), and Mark's about 65 A.D. Before the Gospels there must have been a number of documents relating to Jesus' miracles, parables, teachings, activities and personal memories of many people. Matthew, Mark and Luke must have sifted through all that was available to them.

Chapter 1 Zechariah & Elizabeth are to have a son. Zechariah cannot believe it. He is struck dumb. Mary is invited by God to be the mother of his son. Mary visits Elizabeth. John the Baptist is born, and his father praises God.

Chapter 2 Jesus is born at Bethlehem. The shepherds (representing the Old Testament great men who were all shepherds – Abraham, Isaac, Jacob, Moses, David) rejoice at the longed-for birth. Jesus presented in the Temple, and Simeon & Anna rejoice. Jesus is lost, and found on the third day – an image of the Resurrection.

Chapter 3 John the Baptist prepares the way for Jesus by his preaching, baptises Jesus and is imprisoned.

Chapter 4 Jesus prepares for his ministry by spending time in the desert – an image of the Israelites in the desert with Moses, preparing to be God's people. Jesus is tempted as the Israelites were. Jesus begins his preaching in his own region. Note that vv 16-30 are three separate visits. Can you see the joins? Jesus begins to heal, including Simon's mother-in-law.

Chapter 5 Jesus calls the first four disciples. Notice how different this account is from those in Matthew and Mark, and John's account is different again. Jesus cures a leper. Jesus heals the paralysed man. (Notice how differently Luke and Matthew and Mark tell this same story). Jesus calls Levi. Is it Matthew? Jesus eats with sinners and does not fast. What sort of religious man is he?

Chapter 6 Jesus' healings and actions causing trouble. He chooses twelve apostles from amongst his disciples. Was there jealousy? Do you remember the names of the Twelve? Verse 17 begins what is called the Sermon of the Plain. Its teachings are similar to the Sermon on the Mount in Matthew's Gospel. Luke & Matthew have grouped together various of Jesus' teachings as though given at one time.

Chapter 7 Jesus' healing ministry continues – the centurion's son (see different versions in Matthew and John), the widow's son. John the Baptist's disciples question him. Jesus praises John. The sinful woman approaches Jesus. She is not named.

Chapter 8 Women amongst Jesus' disciples. Parables of the sower and the lamp. Jesus' family worried about him? Jesus calms a storm, heals a demoniac and the woman with a haemorrhage, raises Jairus' daughter to life.

Chapter 9 The Twelve are sent on a mission. The miracle of the loaves and fishes. Peter inspired to see who Jesus truly is. Carry your cross: Jesus will carry his. Transfiguration. Disciples are jealous of each other and of others.

Chapter 10 Mission of the seventy-two. It goes well. The Good News (Gospel) to everyone. The great commandment, illustrated by the parable of the Good Samaritan and the story of Martha and Mary.

Chapter 11 The Lord's Prayer. Keep praying. A promise. Jesus accused of being in league with the devil. Jesus defends himself against antagonism and Pharisees and lawyers.

Chapter 12 Be open and honest. Don't be covetous. Trust in God. Be generous. Be ready for God's call.

Chapter 13 Repentance. Jesus heals on the Sabbath day. Yeast and mustard seed. Gentiles called by God's love. Jerusalem admonished.

Chapter 14 Another Sabbath healing. Be humble and be generous. The banquet to which people are unwilling to come. Being prepared to renounce family and possessions.

Chapter 15 Parables of the lost: sheep, drachma, son.

Chapter 16 The Crafty Steward, right use of money, the rich man (Dives) and Lazarus.

Chapter 17 Good example, correcting one another, service. Ten Lepers. The signs of the coming of the New Testament and of the end of the world.

Chapter 18 The judge and the widow – keep praying. The Pharisee and the publican (tax collector). Jesus and children. The rich young man. Danger of riches. The blind man of Jericho (Matthew has two).

Chapter 19 Zacchaeus is converted. Strange parable of the pounds. Jesus enters Jerusalem, and weeps over it.

Chapter 20 Jesus is challenged. Parable of the vine-dressers. Tribute to Caesar? Sadducees challenge Jesus on resurrection from the dead.

Chapter 21 The Widow's Mite. Jesus speaks again of the destruction of Jerusalem and of the end of the world.

Chapter 22 Judas ready to betray Jesus. Passover supper is prepared The Supper. Who was there? When was it celebrated? The Eucharist. Disciples still jealous of each other. Peter reassures Jesus of his faithfulness. The arrest in the garden on the Mount of Olives. Peter denies Jesus. Jesus before the Sanhedrin.

Chapter 23 Jesus before Pilate and Herod. Calvary and the Crucifixion. The good thief (only Luke mentions him). Jesus dies and is buried.

Chapter 24 Sunday morning at the tomb. The disciples on the road to Emmaus. They recognise Jesus at the breaking of bread. Were they at the Last Supper? Jesus appears to the Apostles, and explains the Scriptures to them. The Ascension. On the evening of the Resurrection? at Bethany? But Luke says in the Acts of the Apostles it occurred on the Mount of Olives forty days after the Resurrection. And Matthew and John say that Jesus was in Galilee after the Resurrection. Puzzle it out.

Part 10
The Acts of the Apostles &
Apostolic Letters

St Luke wrote the Acts of the Apostles, following on his gospel. Again he dedicates it to Theophilus ("loved by God") who may be you and me – "Dear Reader." Again he has done careful research, and scholars tell us how clear a distinction there is between the style of his sources and his own writing. His Greek tries to reflect the tones of the documents he found: his own writing is fluent and scholarly.

Luke was a close friend of St Paul, and travelled with him on two missionary journeys.

Chapter 1 The Ascension. Compare this account with the one at the end of Luke's Gospel. Why the differences? Matthias elected to take the place of Judas.

Chapter 2 Holy Spirit comes on the feast of Pentecost. Peter speaks to the people. He is filled with the Holy Spirit, and many ask to become Christians. Idealised picture of first Christian community.

Chapter 3 Peter and John cure the man lame from birth. Peter speaks to the surprised crowd about the power of Christ.

Chapter 4 Peter and John arrested and brought before the court. The Christian community rejoices at being persecuted for Christ's sake.

Chapter 5 The deceit of Ananias and Sapphira. The Apostles are arrested again. Gamaliel advises wisely: leave the Christians alone. If their inspiration is of God it should not be opposed; if it is merely human it will fade away.

Chapter 6 Seven deacons are chosen. One of them, Stephen, is arrested.

Chapter 7 Stephen tells the story of Israel, and shows the stubbornness of the people. The people are enraged and stone Stephen to death.

Chapter 8 Persecution breaks out, and the Christians flee for safety. The Word of God comes to Samaria. Simon tries to buy the Apostles' power. Philip baptises the court eunuch. Notice the conversion is immediate.

Chapter 9 Saul is converted, on the road to Damascus. Notice Ananias is bewildered. He thinks God does not understand. Paul preaches for the first time. Peter works miracles.

Chapter 10 Peter realises that Christ's message of God's love is for everyone, not only for the Chosen People. He visits the house of the Roman Centurion, and the first pagans are converted.

Chapter 11 Peter defends himself against narrow-minded Christians. The Church at Antioch is established. Barnabas brings Saul to Antioch, and they both go to Jerusalem.

Chapter 12 Peter is arrested. He escapes prison miraculously.

Chapter 13 Barnabas and Saul go on their first missionary journey. 'Saul' becomes 'Paul' in v 9, and thereafter. Paul's preaching traces the story of Israel down to Jesus who has risen from the dead – some accept, some reject, his good news.

Chapter 14 Paul heals the cripple. Paul and Barnabas seen as gods. The mission continues.

Chapter 15 The Council of Jerusalem – the first of the 20 Ecumenical Councils of the Church. Its central question is: should Christians, especially Gentile converts, be held to the law of Moses? Peter and Paul on opposing sides. Paul wins. James speaks as head of the Church at Jerusalem. Apostolic letter sent to the Churches. Barnabas and Paul quarrel and separate.

Chapter 16 Paul's second Missionary journey, through Asia Minor. Like Peter, he is imprisoned and escapes miraculously.

Chapter 17 The Jews make things difficult for Paul and his companions. Paul speaks to the people of Athens about "the Unknown God" and rising from the dead.

Chapter 18 Church at Corinth established.

Chapter 19 Church at Ephesus established. John the Baptist's disciples given the Holy Spirit. Paul causes the silversmith's riot by undermining worship of Diana.

Chapter 20 Sad farewell to Church at Ephesus.

Chapter 21 Journey to Jerusalem. Paul is arrested.

Chapter 22 Paul tells his story to Jerusalem. The people want to kill him. Paul tells the centurion that he is a Roman citizen.

Chapter 23 Paul before the Sanhedrin. He splits the Pharisees and Sadducees by proclaiming his belief in the resurrection. Conspirators plan to kill him. His nephew reports the plot to the authorities. Paul moved to safety.

Chapter 24 Paul before the Roman governor, Felix, whose wife is a Jew, Drusilla. She had left her husband to marry Felix.

Chapter 25 Paul appeals to Caesar, and the new governor, Festus, agrees he must go to Rome. But he is puzzled, and brings Paul before King Agrippa and Bernice.

Chapter 26 Paul speaks convincingly. Agrippa is shaken. Festus is startled.

Chapter 27 Paul goes to Rome as a prisoner. A journey of storm and shipwreck.

Chapter 28 A safe haven in Malta. The people make Paul welcome. Paul reaches Rome.

Letters of the Apostles – James, Peter, John, Jude.

James writes for Jewish converts familiar with the Old Testament – **1** Put up with trials, be strong under temptation, do good. **2** Love the poor. Believe in God, and express your belief in good works. **3** Guard your tongue and be wise. **4** Don't quarrel and be divisive. **5** Be just to one another, help each other, pray for one another.

1 Peter – 1 Our joy in the Risen Christ, the hope of the prophets. Be holy, and love one another. **2** Be people of integrity, we share the priesthood of Christ. Remember obligations towards unbelievers, civil authority, and slaves to master. **3** Be faithful and considerate in marriage, be kind to one another, accept antagonism for the sake of Christ. **4** Lead pure lives. Christ is near. **5** Instructions to elders and faithful.

2 Peter – 1 Christian living. Apostolic witness speaks of the Risen Christ. **2** Beware false teachers, especially those who would lead you to immoral living. **3** Our time, God's time. Live holy and saintly lives.

1 John – 1 We have seen God's Incarnate Word. Live in his light. **2** Keep the commandments. Beware of worldly attractions. Be aware of the enemies of Christ. **3** As God's children finish with sin, keep the commandments, love one another. **4** Beware of the enemies of Christ. Love comes from God. Live and share it. **5** Have faith, we share eternal life. Pray for sinners. We all belong to God.

2 John – Love one another. Beware of Christ's enemies.

3 John – You are kind. We share God's work.

Jude – We share Christ's salvation. But there are false teachers, and you must guard against their speaking and their behaviour. Love and be thoughtful for one another.

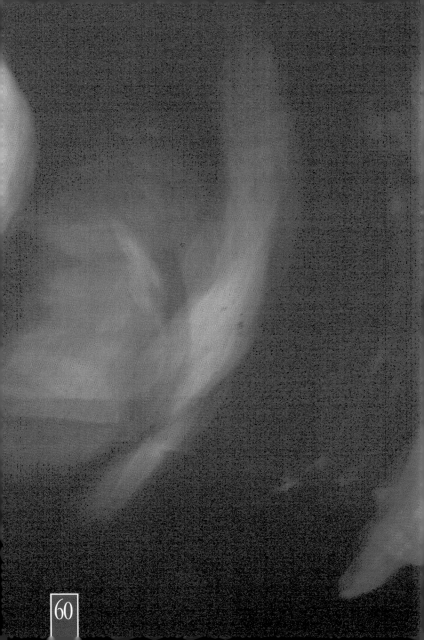

Part 11
The Gospel according to St John

This Gospel was probably written at the beginning of the second century by John's disciples. They based it on his preaching and, probably, on an earlier written account by him. The disciples call John "the disciple Jesus loved" and tell us at the end how hard it had been to select what to write – they could have written books to fill the world.

Chapter 1 The Prologue is wonderful. Its first word is 'Genesis' – "in the beginning" – and echoes the first word of the first book of the Bible. This is a new creation, a new beginning. Jesus is divine, eternal, and sent by God. John the Baptist is his herald. John gives witness to Jesus. The First disciples are called – Andrew and John. They had been followers of the Baptist. The other disciples are called. Notice Nathaniel – his name means "God has given" and he is a true Israelite – he may be a symbol of the true disciple, of all of us.

Chapter 2 The wedding of Cana. Six becomes seven, water becomes wine, wine becomes Eucharist. Old Testament Law (water) becomes New Testament Law (wine, precious Blood). Jesus does it for Mary and the disciples believe in him. Jesus cleanses the Temple, and gives an image of the resurrection.

Chapter 3 Nicodemus comes secretly to speak to Jesus. He cannot understand "being born again". John the Baptist speaks of Jesus.

Chapter 4 Jesus meets the woman at the well. She symbolises the Samaritan people, rejected by the Jews, but loved by Jesus. He wins her patiently, accepting her reaction to him. He stays in Sychar for two days. On the third day he leaves for Galilee, and another miracle – the nobleman's son is cured.

Chapter 5 Jesus cures a sick man at the pool of Bethzatha. It happens on the Sabbath, and the Jewish authorities are angered. Jesus calls God his father, and thus claims to be divine and God's equal. The Jews want to kill such a blasphemer, but Jesus says he speaks the truth.

Chapter 6 Miracle of the loaves and fishes. Jesus walks on the water. He is the new Moses, feeding the people, creating dry land on water. Jesus is the bread of life. How can he give his flesh to be eaten? Peter professes his faith.

Chapter 7 Jesus teaches in Jerusalem. His teaching comes from God. He is Messiah? He will not be with them much longer. No-one has ever spoken as he does.

Chapter 8 The woman taken in adultery. Jesus forgives her. Did her husband and children and neighbours? Jesus is light of the world. The people are unbelieving. Jesus says they are not truly of God, nor even of Abraham, because they want to kill him.

Chapter 9 Jesus cures the man born blind – image of the Gentiles who have never known (seen) God. Jewish authorities are angry that the man (Gentile) praises Jesus.

Chapter 10 The good shepherd. Under challenge in Jerusalem Jesus claims to be the Son of God. They say he blasphemes.

Chapter 11 Resurrection of Lazarus. Notice that Jesus waits two days after receiving the message from Mary and Martha. He moves on the third day. There is resurrection. The authorities decide to kill Jesus.

Chapter 12 Mary anoints Jesus at Bethany. John says it is six days before the Passover. But Marks says it happened two days before. When was the Passover? Were there two celebrations? Yes, probably. Jesus celebrated on the Tuesday with his followers, according to the solar calendar they used: and Jerusalem celebrated on the Saturday, according to the lunar calendar they used. Jesus enters Jerusalem. He talks about his approaching death.

Chapter 13 The Last Supper. Washing of Apostles' feet. Judas's treachery. The new commandment – love as Jesus does.

Chapter 14 Heaven – to see Jesus is to see the Father. Promise of the sending of the Holy Spirit, the Advocate, the Paraclete.

Chapter 15 Jesus is the vine, we are the branches. We must bear fruit. The world will hate Jesus' disciples.

Chapter 16 Coming of the Spirit. Jesus will return soon. Jesus speaking more plainly.

Chapter 17 Jesus offers himself to the Father. He is sacrifice and priest. He prays for his disciples.

Chapter 18 Jesus arrested in the garden. Brought before Annas and Caiaphas. Peter denies Jesus. Jesus before Pilate.

Chapter 19 Jesus condemned to die. The crucifixion. Christ's garments shared out. He speaks to Mary and John. He is pierced. He is buried.

Chapter 20 The Resurrection. Mary tells Peter and John. John sees and believes. What does he see? Jesus appears to Mary Magdalene Jesus appears to his disciples. Thomas does not believe. Then he does.

Chapter 21 Jesus appears on the shore of the Sea of Galilee. Miraculous catch of fish – bread & fish for a meal. 153 fish caught. Peter given his chance to affirm his love for Jesus – three affirmations cancel three denials. Notice the final words: they are written by John's disciples.

Part 12
Book of Revelation
or of the
Apocalypse

This is a strange book and difficult to understand – because of its style of writing, with fantastic pictures, vivid images, and profound ideas. It was written in time of persecution to bring hope and to reassure believers that God was with them and the persecution would pass. The Early Church received it as written by the apostle John.

Chapter 1 John greets the seven churches of Asia. He has had a vision of God, and received messages for the churches.

Chapter 2 Ephesus should return to its former fervour. Smyrna must stay faithful. Pergamum is not so faithful as before. In Thyatira the prophetess Jezebel is leading people astray.

Chapter 3 Faith is fading in Sardis. Philadelphia has stayed faithful. Laodicea is the least faithful of the churches.

Chapter 4 A strange vision of Heaven.

Chapter 5 God gives a scroll to the Lamb of God. The Lamb had suffered and was worthy to open the scroll.

Chapter 6 The Lamb breaks the scroll's seals one by one. There are strange consequences.

Chapter 7 God's people to be protected. The saints are safe.

Chapter 8 Silence, and then four of seven trumpets are sounded. There are frightening consequences.

Chapter 9 Trumpets five and six are sounded. Terrifying images of suffering on earth.

Chapter 10 Not yet the time for full understanding. The prophet eats a small scroll, and must prophesy.

Chapter 11 Peter and Paul are the two witnesses. The seventh trumpet is sounded, and God's time has come.

Chapter 12 The woman is Israel, the Church, and the baby is the Messiah, Jesus. The dragon is the power of evil, Satan.

Chapter 13 The beast is Satan's representative on earth. It is

Rome and its empire: seven emperors and ten kings (see chapter 17).

Chapter 14 The Lamb and his companions. The angels announce the good news. Happy are those who die in the Lord. The sickle marks the end of time.

Chapter 15 Seven angels bring seven plagues **16** and they are spilled over the earth. The plagues recall Moses in Egypt.

Chapter 17 Babylon (Rome) is punished. The power of Rome will be destroyed.

Chapter 18 The peoples of the world mourn for Babylon (Rome), but God's people are invited away to safety.

Chapter 19 Rejoicing in Heaven, followed by an extraordinary battle between Good and Evil.

Chapter 20 The Reign of a thousand years, followed by the second and final battle, and the Final Judgement.

Chapter 21 The heavenly Jerusalem. God speaks from his throne. A vision of the heavenly Jerusalem.

Chapter 22 The river of life flows through the Eternal City. The angel speaks, John speaks, Jesus speaks.

Story in the Bible

Story can reveal truth as fully as history or fact. A good story or film or play reflects human life and its understanding and can touch us deeply.

Yet people can feel uncomfortable at 'story' in the Bible, as though it were a second-class way of God's expressing his truth. To say that the story of Man and Woman at the beginning of the Bible is myth (a story that reveals religious truth) is to say it is untrue, for some people. But story is everywhere in the Bible.

Jesus spoke parables, simple stories holding moral and religious truth. Nathan the prophet told the story of a rich farmer and a poor man to arouse David's sense of guilt. The

Song of Songs is a love story to express God's love for his people.
And there are Books which are stories.

Book of Genesis

The opening chapters are story, but they convey powerful
religious truths. God is the Creator of the world. He created
everything good. But mankind brought evil into God's world
("they ate the fruit of the tree of the knowledge of good and
evil"), destroyed their own wonderful relationship of oneness
and equality, and saw brother kill brother. It was the world the
author knew – evil following evil. The sad prologue to the story
of Abraham and the Chosen People is a story of God's good
creation spoiled by human sin.

Books of Tobit, Judith, Esther

These tell of people faithful to God in frightening circumstances,
never losing faith and trust in him. **Tobit** is blinded, but
continues to live his good life. He guides his son to manhood,
encourages him to seek a God-fearing wife, and is healed at
the end of the story when his son returns happily home with
his new wife. All through the story God's love and providence
are strong.

Judith is an intelligent woman who brings deliverance to her
beleaguered city. Her fellow citizens have almost lost faith in
God. She chides them, and says God will help her bring them
deliverance. Her simple clever plot works perfectly, and the
city is free. Trust in God is the lesson of the book.

Esther is the beautiful queen of King Ahasuerus. Her uncle
Mordecai tells her of a plot to exterminate the Jews, and pleads
with her to approach the king. She prays for two days, and on
the third day she approaches the king. He listens, the people
are safe, and God has answered her prayer.

Books of Job and Jonah

The Book of Job is an exploration of the mystery of human suffering. Job is a good man, yet suffers much. There is no answer, yet. A powerful drama, full of the pain of non-understanding.

Jonah is a narrow-minded selfish prophet, wanting God's blessing and forgiveness only for the Chosen People. God pleads with him to speak of God's love for the people of Nineveh. The book is part of the debate within Judaism on God's love: is it only for the Chosen People, or is it also for the whole world?

Birth of Jesus in the Gospel according to St Matthew and St Luke

The first chapters of these two Gospels are best read as beautiful story, opening out the themes of the salvation that Jesus brought to the people of Israel and to the world. The chapters are full of echoes of Old and New Testament, and written to reflect Christian meditation on what Jesus was and what his birth has meant to the world.

Published by
Redemptorist Publications
Alphonsus House Chawton Alton Hampshire GU34 3HQ

Text: John Daley
Design: Roger Smith

Photography: Cover, Dead Sea Scroll.
David Toase: Pages 6&7, 11, 15, 19, 24, 30&31, 60&61, 65
Alex Gillespie:Pages 48&49
The Phillips Collection: Page 54
David Alexander: Pages 42&43
Fiona Alison: Page 37

First Printed   August 1996

ISBN 0 85231 158 3

Printed by: Bourne Press Limited Bournemouth BH1 4QA